4 45

PowerKids Readers:

My World of Science™

Bilingual Edition
English/Spanish
Edición bilingüe

Wedges in My World
Cuñas en mi mundo

Joanne Randolph

Traducción al español: María Cristina Brusca

The Rosen Publishing Group's
PowerKids Press™ & Editorial Buenas Letras™
New York

For Linda Lou and Lucas

Published in 2006 by The Rosen Publishing Group, Inc.
29 East 21st Street, New York, NY 10010

First Edition

Photo Credits: Cover and pp. 15, 22 (hull) © Robert Essel NYC/Corbis; Cover and p. 17 © Michael Freeman/Corbis; Cover and pp. 5, 9 © Royalty-Free/Corbis; pp. 7, 22 (inclined plane) © Patrick Ward/Corbis; pp. 11, 22 (blade) © Dale C. Spartas/Corbis; p. 13 © Lew Robertson/Corbis; pp. 19, 22 (doorstop) Maura B. McConnell; p. 21 © Charlie Munsey/Corbis; p. 22 (ramp) © Mike McQueen/Corbis.

Library of Congress Cataloging-in-Publication Data

Randolph, Joanne.
[Wedges in my world. Spanish & English] Wedges in my world = Cuñas en mi mundo / Joanne Randolph ; traducción al español, María Cristina Brusca.— 1st ed.
p. cm. — (My world of science)
Includes bibliographical references and index. ISBN 1-4042-3322-9 (library binding)
1. Wedges—Juvenile literature. I. Title.
TJ1201.W44R 2006
621.8'11—dc22
2005005975

Manufactured in the United States of America

Contents

Contenido

A wedge is a simple machine. People use simple machines to help them do work. A wedge is used to push things apart.

Una cuña es una máquina simple. La gente usa máquinas simples que la ayudan a trabajar. Las cuñas se usan para separar cosas.

5

A wedge is a kind of inclined plane. A ramp is an inclined plane. It stays in one place to be used. A wedge is two inclined planes together.

Una cuña es un tipo de plano inclinado. Una rampa es un plano inclinado. Una rampa está fija en un lugar. Una cuña está formada por dos planos inclinados.

inclined plane
plano inclinado

7

A wedge has a pointed end.
This pointed end of a wedge
can be fit in between
objects. When the wedge is
moved the objects are
pushed apart.

La cuña tiene un extremo en
forma de punta. Esta punta se
puede meter entre dos objetos.
Cuando la cuña se mueve los
objetos se separan en
direcciones opuestas.

The blade of an ax is a wedge. People use axes to chop down trees or to split wood. A person swings the ax to give the wedge power.

La hoja de un hacha es una cuña. La gente usa hachas para cortar árboles o partir leña. La persona balancea el hacha para darle fuerza a su cuña.

A knife is a wedge, too. A knife is a bit wider at the top edge. The thin bottom edge is called the blade. The blade is the name for the edge of the wedge.

El cuchillo es también una cuña. La hoja del cuchillo es un poco más ancha en la parte de arriba. El borde delgado que está abajo se llama filo. El filo es una cuña.

The bow of a boat is a wedge. Its shape allows the boat to cut through the water easily. If the front of a boat were flat, it would take more work to push through the water.

La proa de un barco es una cuña. Su forma le permite cortar el agua fácilmente. Si la proa fuera plana, al barco le costaría más trabajo moverse en el agua.

A plow is another wedge. Its shape allows it to cut through the earth. Farmers use plows to help them do their work.

El arado es otra cuña. Su forma le permite cortar la tierra. Los arados ayudan a los granjeros en su trabajo.

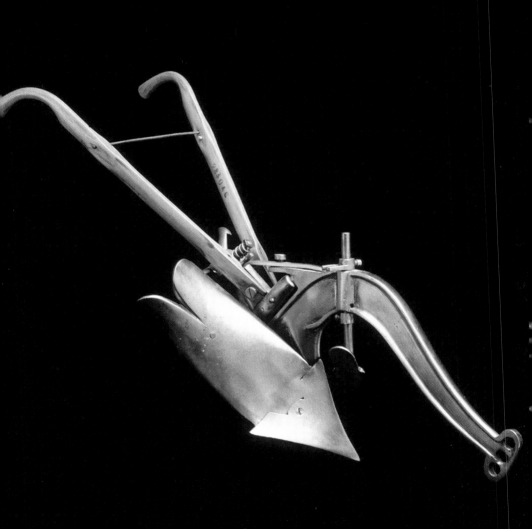

17

A doorstop is a wedge, too. A doorstop is not used to push things apart, though. It uses its special shape to keep a door from moving.

Un tope de puerta es también una cuña. Sin embargo el tope de puerta no se usa para apartar cosas. Su forma especial se usa para no permitir que la puerta se mueva.

Can you think of wedges you see around you? Look at this picture. Can you find the wedge here?

¿Puedes pensar en otras cuñas que se vean a tu alrededor? Mira esta foto. ¿Dónde se encuentra la cuña?

Words to Know
Palabras que debes saber

blade
hoja

bow
proa

doorstop
tope de puerta

inclined plane
plano inclinado

ramp
rampa

Here are more books to read about wedges:
Otros libros que puedes leer sobre cuñas:

In English/En inglés
Ramps and Wedges (Useful Machines)
by Chris Oxlade
Heinemann Library, 2003

Bilingual (English-Spanish)/Bilingüe (Inglés-Español)
*Cómo podemos utilizar la cuña/How Can I
Experiment With Simple Machines: the Wedge*
by David Armentrout and Patricia Armentrout
Rourke Publishing, 2002

Web Sites/En Internet
Due to the changing nature of Internet links,
PowerKids Press and Editorial Buenas Letras have
developed an online list of Web sites related to the
subject of this book. This site is updated regularly.
Please use this link to access the list:

www.powerkidslinks.com/mws/wedges/

Index

A
ax, 10

B
blade, 10, 12
bow, 14

D
doorstop, 18

K
knife, 12

M
machine, 4

P
plow, 16

Índice

A
arado, 16

C
cuchillo, 12

H
hacha, 10
hoja, 10, 12

P
proa, 14

M
máquina, 4

T
tope de puerta, 18

Word Count: 250

Número de palabras: 248

Note to Librarians, Teachers, and Parents

PowerKids Readers are specially designed to help emergent and beginning readers build their skills in reading for information. Sentences are short and simple, employing a basic vocabulary of sight words, simple vocabulary, and basic concepts, as well as new words that describe objects or processes that relate to the topic. Large type, clean design, and stunning photographs corresponding directly to the text all help children to decipher meaning. Features such as a contents page, picture glossary, and index introduce children to the basic elements of a book, which they will encounter in their future reading experiences.